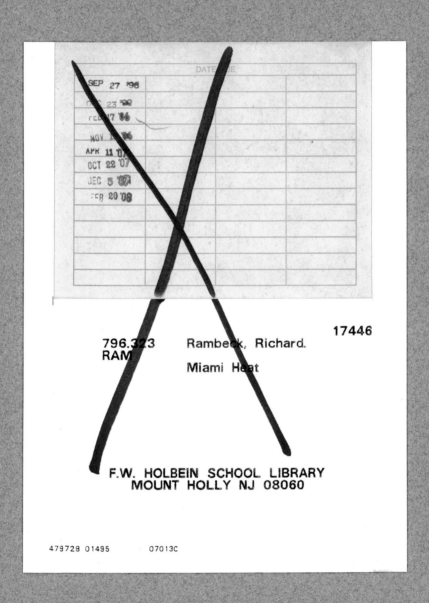

MIAMI HEAT

RICHARD RAMBECK

COVER AND TITLE PAGE PHOTOS BY MATT MAHURIN

CREATIVE EDUCATION

Published by Creative Education, Inc.
123 S. Broad Street, Mankato, Minnesota 56001 USA

Art Director, Rita Marshall
Cover and title page photography by Matt Mahurin
Book design by Rita Marshall

Photos by: Allsport; Mel Bailey; Bettmann Archive;
Brian Drake; Duomo; Focus On Sports; FPG; Photo
by Sissac; South Florida Images Inc.; Spectra-Action;
Sportschrome; Sports Photo Masters, Inc.; SportsLight:
Brian Drake, Long Photography; Wide World Photos.

Library of Congress Cataloging-in-Publication Data

Rambeck, Richard.

Miami Heat / Richard Rambeck.

Summary: A history of the NBA expansion team
which began playing in Miami, Florida, during the
1988-89 season.

ISBN 0-88682-561-X

1. Miami Heat (Basketball team)—History—Juvenile
literature. [1. Miami Heat (Basketball team)—History.
2. Basketball—History.] I. Title.

GV885.52.M53R36 1992   92-3169

796.323'64'09759381—dc20   CIP

MIAMI: HOME OF THE HEAT

Located on the southeastern coast of the state of Florida, Miami is one of the vacation capitals of the United States. Tourists come from all over the country to enjoy Miami's beaches, sunny climate, hot temperatures, and huge waterfront hotels. Over the years, the area's climate and luxurious accommodations have also prompted many wealthy families and show-business personalities to establish vacation homes there.

With Miami's reputation for sun and fun, it's only natural that the city has a love affair with sports. Individual sports such as tennis and golf are very popular among Miami residents. Miamians also have a passion for watching team sports. The city has hosted college football's Orange Bowl

Team mascot Burnie adds to the fun.

since 1935, and the local University of Miami Hurricanes always rank among college football's best teams. The Miami Dolphins have been playing pro football in jam-packed stadiums since 1967. And the Florida Marlins, an expansion baseball franchise in the National League, will begin playing in Miami in 1993.

By the time the Marlins take to the diamond, another new professional sports franchise in the area hopes to be contending for the championship of the National Basketball Association. The Miami Heat, which made its NBA debut in the 1988-89 season, has been slowly but surely improving year by year. Since the day the franchise was awarded to Miami by the NBA, its management has been committed to finding and developing young players, and to building a successful team.

In August 1986, builders broke ground on Miami Arena, the Heat's new home.

BRINGING THE HEAT TO HOT MIAMI

The drive to establish an NBA expansion team in Miami began on May 6, 1986. A group of men with vastly different backgrounds held a press conference to announce their plans to bring professional basketball to Florida's largest city. One of those men was Billy Cunningham, a former NBA All-Star and former coach of the Philadelphia 76ers. Cunningham, who had moved to Florida, wanted to be involved in the NBA again, but not as a coach. He didn't have enough money, however, to own a team by himself. He needed partners with deep pockets to add their wealth to his investment, and he found them.

The first wealthy businessman to join Cunningham's project was Zev Bufman. Bufman didn't have any basketball experience at all. Born in Israel, Bufman came to the

Center Rony Seikaly soars for two.

The Heat's 10,000th season ticket holder signed up on Christmas Eve, 1987.

United States in 1952 and eventually became a successful producer of plays on Broadway. When he heard about Cunningham's idea, Bufman jumped at the chance. "I thought it was time South Florida had a basketball team," Bufman explained. "Besides, I got tired of watching basketball on TV or having to go to Los Angeles or New York to see a game."

Cunningham and Bufman then approached Ted Arison, who had built successful empires in shipping, air cargo, and cruise-ship lines. At the time, Arison was chairman of Hamilton Holdings, a company that managed real estate all over the southeastern United States. He had never seen a professional basketball game, but he was more than willing to become a partner. "For what it means to the city, it's all worth it," Arison said.

With Arison on board, Cunningham turned to a childhood friend, Lewis Schaffel, for support. Cunningham and Schaffel had been buddies since they were eight years old. Unlike Bufman and Arison, Schaffel had a strong basketball background. He was then serving as chief operating officer of the New Jersey Nets, and was a former general manager of the New Orleans Jazz.

When Cunningham called, Schaffel accepted his offer to join the Miami expansion project. Schaffel immediately became the managing partner of the franchise. One of his first duties was finding a nickname for the club. He held a contest in which there were 20,000 entries. Team officials chose "Heat" as the nickname, which was fitting both because of the usually hot Miami climate and because of the heated excitement the owners hoped their new team would generate among Miami basketball fans.

BUILDING A TEAM WITH DEFENSE

With its nickname determined, the Miami franchise next needed to find a coach and to choose its first group of players. Schaffel had his eye on Ron Rothstein, the top assistant coach for the Detroit Pistons, to lead the team. Rothstein had helped Piston head coach Chuck Daly design a defensive strategy that made Detroit one of the best teams in the NBA. After the Pistons lost to the Los Angeles Lakers in the 1987-88 league championship series, Schaffel called Rothstein and asked him to come to Miami. Rothstein, who had been an NBA assistant coach for several years, leaped at the chance to be a head coach.

Just six years before taking over the Heat, Ron Rothstein was coaching high school in Eastchester, New York.

The Heat's new leader knew that his club wouldn't be successful right away, but he was willing to allow the team the time it needed to develop. "You've got to be patient with your players," Rothstein explained. "They are going to make mistakes. The thing I want to stress is that we want to get better every time we step on the court. Shortcuts lead down the road to failure."

Rothstein wasn't planning to take any shortcuts when it came to defense. He was determined to mold the Miami team into a low-scoring, defense-minded, hustling club similar to the one he had helped build in Detroit.

Schaffel, Cunningham, and Rothstein agreed that the team's foundation would be constructed with young college and pro stars, not NBA veterans in the declining years of their careers. The Heat would get players from two sources: the college draft and the NBA expansion draft. In the expansion draft, teams were allowed to "protect" eight of the 12 players on their rosters. One of the remaining

One of Miami's young stars, Willie Burton.

The hustling Alec Kessler.

November 5, 1988: Rory Sparrow sank the Heat's first field goal one minute into the team's first game.

four players on each team could be drafted by the Heat or by the Charlotte Hornets, the other expansion franchise that would begin play in 1988-89.

The Heat had a master plan for the expansion draft. Team officials decided to use it to gather as many choices in the 1988 college draft as possible. When the expansion draft started, the Heat startled the experts by announcing the selection of Dallas forward Arvid Kramer, a player few in the league had even heard of. But Miami got more than Kramer from Dallas. The Heat also received the Mavericks' first-round choice in the college draft in return for picking Kramer instead of any of the other unprotected Dallas players.

The Heat also received second-round draft choices from the Boston Celtics for not taking veteran guard Dennis Johnson and from the Los Angeles Lakers for not selecting center Kareem Abdul-Jabbar. Both potential Hall-of-Famers were left unprotected by their teams. When the dealing was done, Miami had five picks among the first 40 choices of the college draft—two first-rounders and three second-rounders.

Kevin Edwards was the team's number-two draft pick but its number-one scorer in 1988-89.

The Heat used both of its first-round picks wisely. The team selected Syracuse center Rony Seikaly with its initial opening-round choice. Then, with the pick received from Dallas, Miami drafted Kevin Edwards, a 6-foot-5 guard from DePaul University. Miami also got a hidden gem in the second round when the club selected Grant Long, a 6-foot-9, 230-pound forward from Eastern Michigan.

CENTERING THE FUTURE ON SEIKALY

Of the team's three top picks, both Edwards and Long got off to quicker starts than did Seikaly. But team officials knew that the young 7-foot center was the team's major building block for the future. Seikaly was a talent who needed more time to develop. In fact, he was still learning the game. Born in Lebanon and schooled in Greece, Seikaly didn't start playing basketball until after his junior year in high school.

When he enrolled at Syracuse, Seikaly showed limited basketball skills, but he was obviously a good all-around athlete. By the time his college career ended, Seikaly had

On January 10, 1989, Rony Seikaly recorded Miami's first 30-point performance, outdueling Utah's Mark Eaton.

developed into one of the top talents in the country, though he still had a few weaknesses. "Offensively, he's not as fluid as you'd like him to be, and he fouls a lot," said Marty Blake, chief scout of the NBA. "But he's aggressive, he's smart, and he can run."

Seikaly was prepared to work as hard as he could to improve. "I know I'm a long way from what great players are," he admitted. "I have to stay out of foul trouble and learn to pass better. There's a lot I have to learn."

Once the 1988-89 season started, it was obvious that the entire Heat squad had a lot to learn in order to become a good team. Miami set an NBA record by losing its first 16 games. The team was relying on inexperienced rookies and a small core of veterans who were acquired in the expansion draft. The veterans included point guard Rory Sparrow, forward Billy Thompson, and shooting guard Jon Sundvold. The three players provided leadership for their younger teammates, but they couldn't inspire the club to victory. Miami finally broke the ice on December 14, 1988, with an 89-88 win over the Los Angeles Clippers in the L.A. Sports Arena.

Despite the team's struggles, the Miami fans and the Miami media remained supportive. The fans kept filling Miami's 15,000-seat arena even though the team wound up with the worst record in the league during the 1988-89 season (15-67). "There's truly a love affair between the fans and the players," said team co-owner Zev Bufman. One of the players, Jon Sundvold, made a promise to the team's loyal supporters. "We'll be much better next season," he said confidently.

1988 second-round pick Grant Long.

Glen Rice outscored all three rookies drafted before him in 1989 (Pervis Ellison, Danny Ferry, and Sean Elliott).

TWO NEW GEMS: RICE AND DOUGLAS

For the Heat to become a better team, the club had to acquire some solid talent in the 1989 college draft. Miami had the fourth choice in the first round, and team officials set their sights on a high-scoring forward from the University of Michigan named Glen Rice. Rice had shot the Wolverines to the 1988-89 NCAA title, breaking an NCAA tournament record by scoring 184 points in six games—more than 30 points a game!

Against Seton Hall in the NCAA title game, Rice poured in 31 points and grabbed 11 rebounds as Michigan won 80-79 in overtime. "I've never seen such a [shot] release so quick," said an exhausted Andrew Gaze, the Seton Hall player who tried to stop Rice. "What an incredible individual."

High-scoring forward Glen Rice.

Miami looks to outjump the competition .

*Long-range bomber
Jon Sundvold led the
NBA in three-point
shooting in 1988-89,
hitting 52 percent.*

In making Rice the team's number-one choice, Heat officials added an outstanding individual scorer to the club. In the second round of the draft, Miami went for a talented, unselfish team player, point guard Sherman Douglas from Syracuse. Douglas and Rony Seikaly had been college teammates. In 1987, the two players had led Syracuse to the NCAA finals against Indiana. Douglas was brilliant in that game, directing the Syracuse offense and providing clutch scoring. Even though Syracuse lost in the closing seconds, Douglas gained a lot of admirers for his play.

Douglas may have had a great college career—he set an NCAA record for most assists during his three seasons as a starter—but he was not highly regarded by pro scouts. "Too small," said some scouts. "Too slow," or "Can't shoot," proclaimed others. Those were the same criticisms college recruiters had voiced about Douglas when he was in high school. Douglas finally did get a scholarship offer from Syracuse, but he wasn't expected to be a star. He was a point guard, and the Orangemen already had a great point guard, Dwayne "Pearl" Washington.

Washington, however, left school to turn pro after his sophomore year, and Douglas became the Orangemen's floor general. Strangely enough, when Douglas joined the Heat, one of the players he was competing against for a roster spot was Pearl Washington. Once again, the Pearl was expected to beat out Douglas for the point guard spot, but Sherman clearly outplayed his rival during the Heat's preseason camp. Washington was cut, and Douglas was given the starting job. He quickly became the best young point guard in the league.

As a rookie, Sherman Douglas became the first Heat player to score 1,000 points and dish out 500 assists.

Douglas finished the 1989-90 season with an average of 14.3 points and 7.6 assists per game. He was Miami's second-leading scorer and was named to the NBA's All-Rookie first team. But it was his former Syracuse teammate who had the best year among the Miami players. Seikaly, who had averaged 10.9 points and 7 rebounds a game during his rookie season, raised both totals in his second year, topping the Heat in scoring (16.6) and rebounding (10.4). His rebounding average was sixth best in the league.

Seikaly's play was noticed throughout the NBA. He was given the league's Most Improved Player award. For Seikaly, it was just a matter of more experience producing better performances. "I'm not saying that I didn't work hard during my rookie year," he said. "You have to understand that, during my first season, we had players who were rook-

A dramatic ending to a Heat fastbreak.

ies or bench players all their lives. That didn't help my cause in any way. If I had gone to the [Los Angeles] Lakers or any championship team, I would have been brought along slowly. Instead, I was exposed too early."

Another player who might have been exposed too much a little too early was Glen Rice. The rookie first-rounder from Michigan struggled with his shooting throughout the season, but he did manage to finish as Miami's third-leading scorer with a 13.6 average. The highlight of Rice's rookie year was a road game against Utah on March 5, 1990. Trailing the Jazz by one point in the closing seconds of the game, the Heat players got the ball to Rice. With a defender in his face, Rice jumped and launched a long shot. The ball eased through the net with four-tenths of a second to play, and Miami won by a point.

"Iron Man" Grant Long missed just one game during the Heat's first two seasons.

SLOW BUT STEADY IMPROVEMENT

Despite the efforts of Rice, Douglas, and Seikaly, Miami finished with an 18-64 record in its second season. That tied the Heat with the Orlando Magic—the other Florida entry in the NBA—for the second-worst standing in the league. But team officials weren't worried. They knew that their plan for building the club slowly would mean poor records in the early years of the franchise. They were determined to construct the team in stages, letting the young players develop at a gradual pace.

Miami added another potential young star during the 1990 college draft by taking University of Minnesota forward Willie Burton, a high-scoring, long-range shooter in

24   *Left to right: Kevin Edwards, Bimbo Coles, Keith Askins, Dwayne Washington.*

the mold of Glen Rice. The Heat also selected Alec Kessler, a sturdy 6-foot-10 center/forward from the University of Georgia. Kessler, a brilliant student, was planning to go to medical school in addition to playing pro basketball.

With Burton and Kessler added to the roster, the Heat had high hopes of winning as many as 30 games in 1990-91. But injuries hurt the team's chances of improving that much. Seikaly missed almost 20 games. Douglas also suffered through nagging ailments, but the little point guard still managed to have a great year. He raised his scoring average to a club-high 18.5 points a game and also chipped in 8.5 assists per contest. Rice played more minutes than anyone on the team and finished second in scoring with a 17.4 average.

In his senior year at Georgia, Alec Kessler was chosen college basketball's Scholar-Athlete of the Year.

In addition, Willie Burton made the NBA's All-Rookie second team based on his scoring average of 12 points a game. Guard Kevin Edwards tossed in 12.1 points per contest and led the club in steals with 130. And, despite his injuries, Seikaly still averaged 16.4 points and 11.1 rebounds per game. These performances enabled the Heat to finish the 1990-91 season with a 24-58 record, a solid six-game improvement over 1989-90.

Despite the better record, the Heat decided to replace the somewhat inexperienced head coach Ron Rothstein with the very experienced Kevin Loughery before the 1991-92 season. Loughery, who most recently had been an assistant coach with the Atlanta Hawks, had also been a head coach for several NBA teams, including the Hawks, Washington Bullets, and New Jersey Nets. In addition, during the mid-1970s, he had twice led the then-New York Nets to championships in the old American Basketball Association (ABA).

Rony Seikaly has developed into a fine pro center (pages 26-27).

NOT JUST ANY GUY NAMED SMITH

Two years before he became Heat coach in 1991, Kevin Loughery served as one of the team's first scouts.

To help make Loughery's job easier in Miami, the team used its 1991 first-round draft choice to take Steve Smith, a 6-foot-7, 200-pound guard from Michigan State University. Smith, an outstanding all-around player, has been compared at times with another former Michigan State player—Earvin "Magic" Johnson. But Smith doesn't believe he's a newer version of Johnson, although Johnson has been a major influence on him.

"Earvin was one of my heroes," Smith said. "I guess in the back of my mind I always hoped I'd end up playing at Michigan State because of him. Now people ask me if I get tired of being compared to him. Why would anybody get tired of a compliment like that? But I'll never be Magic Smith or anything. I'm just Steve."

Smith has no reason to be modest about his talent. During his college career in East Lansing, Michigan, he was one of the best all-around players in the nation. On any given night, Smith could lead the offense with his passing, or he could control the game with his great shooting and numerous offensive talents. Smith led Michigan State to the Big Ten Conference title during his junior year. It was the school's first league championship in 11 years—since the season when a guard named Magic led the Spartans to Big Ten and NCAA titles.

Smith may not be much of a talker, but he has always been a leader. Growing up in Detroit, Smith and his friends would play basketball on the Smith family's backyard court. "There must have been at least 50 or 60 kids every day, all

ages," recalled Clara Smith, Steve's mother. "Steve did a lot to make sure things didn't get out of hand. There were times I put him out there to control the yard when he was only about 10 years old. There were 18- and 19-year-olds back there playing, but Steve controlled the yard. Sometimes people are surprised that Steve can be so forceful out on the court when he's so quiet the rest of the time. He probably learned that in our backyard."

Smith's role in the club took on great significance at the beginning of his rookie year, when Sherman Douglas and Miami management couldn't reach agreement on a new contract. Douglas sat out the first month of the season, and much of the responsibility for directing the Heat offense fell on Smith's shoulders. Even when Douglas did return, he

Heat newcomer Brian Shaw.

A leader for the 1990s, Steve Smith.

In the last week of the 1991-92 season, the Heat outdueled Atlanta for a berth in the NBA playoffs.

didn't stay long. Within a few weeks, he was sent to Boston in exchange for another young point guard, 6-foot-6 speedster Brian Shaw.

Coach Loughery is depending on Steve Smith's talent and leadership to move the Heat forward in the 1990s. Smith is perhaps the team's most accomplished all-around player: a shooter, a passer, a solid defender, and a leader. He will be expected to inspire the Heat's other young "veterans"—Shaw, Glen Rice, Willie Burton, and Rony Seikaly—to become consistent winners, capable of reaching the playoffs and succeeding in the postseason tournament.

While Loughery considers Smith to be perhaps the club's main ingredient for success in the future, he knows that building a winner involves mixing a team's many different talents together to produce an explosive combination. "We need to develop better team chemistry," the new Miami coach explained. "Talent is the most important thing you need to win in the NBA. But chemistry is right behind it. If we can improve our team chemistry, we can begin to play well not just individually but together as a unit."

Loughery makes no promises about winning a certain number of games, but he also leaves no doubt that he plans to build a team that will fit right in with the winning traditions established by Miami's college and pro football teams. "I'm confident we'll be an exciting team to watch not just this season," Loughery promised, "but in years to come."